Shawno

SHAWNO

by George Dennison

Schocken
Books
·
*New
York*

First published by Schocken Books 1984
10 9 8 7 6 5 4 3 2 1
84 85 86 87

Library of Congress Cataloging in Publication Data
Dennison, George, 1925–
Shawno.
"Originally appeared in The St. John's review
33, no. 2 (1982): 3–23"—T.p. verso.
I. Title.
PS3554.E55S5 1984   813'.54   84–1434

Originally appeared in *The St. John's Review*
33, no. 2 (1982): 3–23.
Designed by Jane Byers Bierhorst
Manufactured in the United States of America
ISBN 0–8052–3917–0

A marathon.
Euphoria. Sights and
sounds in the corridor
of dogs. Finches and
morning.

We could hear our children's voices in the darkness on the sweet-smelling hill by my friend's house, and could hear the barking of Angus, his dog. At nine o'clock Patricia put our three into the car and went home. My friend's wife and son said goodnight shortly afterwards. By then he and I had gone back to the roomy, decrepit, smoke-discolored, homey, extremely pleasant farmhouse kitchen and were finishing the wine we had had at dinner. It was late August. Our northern New England nights would soon make frost, but the cool of the night was still enjoyable. He opened a bottle of *mezcal* he had brought from Mexico, and we talked of the writings of friends, and of the friends themselves, and of our youthful days in New York. He had written a paper on Mahler. We listened to the Eighth and Ninth symphonies, and the unfinished Tenth, which moved him deeply. We talked again. When we parted, the stars, still yellow and numerous in most of the sky, had paled and grown fewer in the east. I set out to walk the four miles home.

I was euphoric, as happens at times, even without *mezcal*. For a short distance, since there was no one to disturb (the town road is a dead-end road and I was at the end of it) I shouted and sang. And truly, for those brief moments, everything did seem right and good, or rather, wonderful and strange. But the echoes of my voice sobered me and I stopped singing. A dog was barking. The night air was moist and cool. I became aware that something was calling for my attention, calling insistently, and then I realized that it was the stream, and so I listened for a while to its noisy bubbling. The lower stars were blocked by densely wooded hills. A dozen or fifteen old houses lay ahead of me still darkened for sleep.

Angus came with me. He is a pointy-nosed, black-and-white mongrel in which border collie predominates, and therefore is bright-eyed and quick-footed, and is amazingly interested in human affairs. He pattered along beside me, turning his head every few seconds to look at me, and it was as if he were keeping up continually a companionable cheerful jabbering. I spoke to him at one point and he barked lightly and jumped toward my face, hoping to kiss me.

Abruptly he sat down. We had come to the edge of what he imagined to be his territory, though in fact we had crossed his line several paces back. He sat there and cocked his head, watching me as I walked away. I had taken only twenty steps when on my right, with jarring suddenness, came the explosive deep barking of the German shepherd tied before the one new house in the valley. Angus sprang up, braced his legs, and hurled his own challenge, that was high-pitched and somewhat frantic, and immediately there came a barking that seemed limitless. I could hear it speeding away into the far distance, dog after dog repeating the challenge. Certainly it passed beyond our village, very likely beyond our state. I was in a corridor of barking dogs.

A soft projectile of some sort spurted from the shadows to my right and came to rest not far from my feet, where it turned out to be a chubby little pug. It was bouncing with excitement, and was giving vent through its open mouth to a continuous siren of indignation. The cluttered porch it had been guarding flared with light. Two elderly spinsters lived here. They rose with the sun, or before it, as did many of the older folk. The clapboards of their house had been a mustard color, the trim of the windows white, but that had been thirty years ago. The barn beside the house had fallen down, the apple trees had decayed, the mound of sheep manure was grassed over. The pug stopped barking and began to wheeze excitedly. It reared up and tapped its tiny paws against my shin, and looked at me out of bulging eyes that seemed adoring and shy. I patted him and scratched his ears.

Twenty paces on I was startled by a barking more savage than that of the shepherd, a murderous, demented screaming that aroused real fear and detestation. He was chained to a dying apple tree before a collapsing gray house on the left side of the road. The hard-packed yard was crowded with wheelless cars. The dog was a Doberman. He leaped at me fiercely, leaped again and again, and was jerked back violently by the chain, as by the hand of a violent master.

Overlapping these disturbing sounds there came the melodious deep tones of the long-legged black hound tied before his own little house in the strange compound farther on: a mobile home, half of a barn, some small sheds, a corral, all huddled before the large trees that bordered the stream. Nothing was finished. There was an air of disconsolate ambition everywhere, failure, and disconsolate endurance. The hound itself seemed disconsolate. He was not tugging at his chain. He had not even braced his feet. He followed me with his eyes, barking his bark that was almost a baying and was actually beautiful. His head was cocked and he seemed to be listening to the other dogs.

What a racket! What a strange, almost musical hullabaloo! I myself was the cause of it, but it wouldn't end when I passed. The sun would be up, the dogs would keep barking, the birds would twitter and chirp, and that wave of noise, of energy and intention, would follow the sun right across the land.

More lights came on. The sun had not yet risen, but the night was gone. It was the morning dusk, fresh

6

and cool. Birds had been calling right along, but now there were more. At intervals I could hear roosters. There were only three. The valley had been noisy once with crowing, and the asphalt road had been an earthen road, packed by wagon wheels and shaded by many elms. The elms were stumps now, huge ones.

Even so, it was beautiful. There were maples and pines beside the road, a few cows were still milked, a few fields were still hayed, a few eggs were still gathered, a few pigs transformed to pork, a few sheep to mutton.

Swallows were darting about. They perched in long rows on the electric wires.

A car passed me from behind, the first.

And Brandy, the Kimbers' gray and ginger mutt, trotted up from the stream and joined me. His hair was bristly, his legs short. He was muscular, energetic, stunted, bearded and mustachioed, like some old campaigner out of the hills of Spain. He went beside me a little way, cheerfully, but without affection. There was no affection in him, but gregarious good cheer and selfish, robust curiosity. He left me to consort with a fluffy collie, who wasn't chained but wouldn't leave its yard. I passed another German shepherd, a chained Husky, an aged cocker spaniel who barked from the doorstep and wouldn't even rise to do it. I came to a small house set back from the road by a small yard. A huge maple overspread the yard. Beneath the maple there stood a blue tractor, a large orange skidder, a pickup truck, two cars, a row-

7

boat, a child's wagon, several bikes. A large, lugubrious Saint Bernard, who all summer had suffered from the heat, was chained to the tree, and she barked at me perfunctorily in a voice not unlike the hound's, almost a baying, but it wasn't a challenge bark at all, or much of one. She wanted to be petted, she wanted to lie down and be scratched, she wanted anything but to hurl a challenge . . . nevertheless, she barked; it would be shameful not to. I came to a Boxer, tied; a purebred border collie, tied; a rabbit hound, tied; several mongrels, not tied, but clustered and apparently waiting for their breakfasts. One, a black, squat hound, had a lame foot and a blind eye, mementos of a terrible mid-winter fight with a fox in defense of newborn pups, who froze to death anyway. She barked vociferously, but then ambled out to apologize and be petted. How fabulous our hands must seem to these fingerless creatures! What pleased surprises we bring to their brows, their throats and backs and bellies, touching as no dog can touch another dog . . .

At almost every house there was a dog. At absolutely every house with a garden there was a dog. One must have one to raise food, or the woodchucks take it all. A second car passed me. My euphoria was abating to good cheer and I was hungry.

The turn to my own road was close now. In the crook of the turn there was a trailer, a so-called mobile home, covered with a second roof of wood. There were three small sheds around it, and a large garden out back, handsome now with the dark greens of po-

8

tato plants and the lighter greens of bush beans. Near the garden were stakes and boxes for horseshoe pitching. A few steps away, at the edge of the stream, there were chairs, benches, and a picnic table. Two battered cars and a battered truck crowded the dooryard, in which there was also a tripod, taller than the trailer, made of strong young maples from the nearby woods. From its apex dangled a block and chain. Bantam hens were scratching the dirt near an aluminum canoe, against which three paddles and four inexpensive fishing rods were leaning. Swimming suits and orange life vests hung from a clothesline. The house was silent. All had watched TV until late at night and all were still asleep, among them my seven-year-old daughter's new-found friend. The uproar of dogs was considerable here. Six were in residence, more or less. The young German shepherd was chained. The handsome Boxer was free; in fact all the others were free, and with one exception ran to upbraid me and greet me. The exception, the incredibly pretty, positively magnetizing exception was Princess, the malamute, who did not bark or move. She lay at her royal ease atop a grassy mound that once had been an elm, her handsome wolf-like head erect and one paw crossed demurely and arrogantly over the other. Her slanted almond-shaped eyes were placed close together and gave her an almost human oriental-slavic air. It was as if she knew she was being admired. She followed me impassively with those provocative eyes, disdaining to respond. How strange she was! She knew me

9

well. If I went near her she'd suddenly melt. She'd sit up and lift one paw tremblingly as high as her head in a gesture of adulation and entreaty. She'd lay her head to one side and let it fall closer and closer to her shoulder in a surrender irresistible in its abject charm—"I am yours, yours utterly"—as if pulling the weight of a lover down on top of her. She ends on her back at such times, belly exposed, hind legs opened wide, lips pulled back voluptuously and front paws tucked under in the air. Especially in the winter, when she alone of the six dogs is allowed into the lamplight of the little home, she indulges in such tricks. The place is overheated. There are times when everyone seems glassy with contentment, and times when bad humor, apparently passing over into bad character, seems hopeless and destructive, and there are quarrels as fierce as the fights of cats. But peace comes again, usually by the intervention of Betsy, the mother, who is mild and benign. She has lost her front teeth and can't afford dentures, yet never hesitates to smile. The children drink soda pop and watch TV, while Verne, who is deep-voiced and patriarchal, with the broad back and muscular huge belly of a Sumo wrestler, sits at the kitchen table sipping beer from a can, measuring gunpowder on a little balance scale, loading and crimping shotgun shells and glancing at the program on the tube. He is opinionated, vain, and egotistical, to the point of foolish pomposity, but he is good-natured and earnest and is easily carried away into animation, and then the posturing vanishes. He issues an order, directs a booming word to one of the kids or dogs, but especially to Princess, who draws effusions one would not think were in him. "Well, Princess!" he roars, "Ain't you the charmer! Ain't you my baby! Ain't you now! Oh, you want your belly scratched? Well, we all do, Princess! We all do! But you're the one that gits it, ain't you! Oh, yes you are! oh, yes!"

This morning I didn't stop to caress the malamute. At the turn in the road I heard a far-off barking that made me smile and want to be home. I crossed the cement bridge and turned into a small dirt road. There wouldn't be a house now for a mile, and then there would be ours and the road would end.

Day had begun. There was color in the sky. The moisture in the air was thinning.

The land was flat and paralleled the stream, which was to my right now. Here and there along its banks, in May, after the flood has gone down and the soil has warmed, we gather the just-emerging coils of the ferns called fiddleheads. Occasionally I have fished here, not really hopefully (the trout are few), but because the stream is so exciting. Once, however, while I knelt on the bank baiting my hook, I glanced into the water, deep at that point, and saw gliding heavily downstream a fish I scarcely could believe to be a trout. What a passion of helplessness seized me! I would have jumped on it bodily if that might have succeeded. I learned later that ice had broken the dam to a private fishpond in the hills and this prize and many others had escaped down tributaries to the main stream and the river.

To my left, beyond a miniature bog of alders and swale lay a handsome small pond. Its outlet joined the stream fifty yards on, flowing under a bridge of stout pine stringers and heavy planks. The game warden had been here several times with dynamite, but the beavers had rebuilt their dam across the outlet, and once again the pond was eighteen inches higher than the stream. It was not unusual to see them. They had cut their half-tunnels under all these banks, creating concave, overhanging edges. I had stood here with the children one night, downstream from the bridge, at the water's edge, looking for beavers, and two had passed under our feet. It was a windless mellow night of full moon. I saw the glint of moonlight on the beaver's fur as he emerged from his channel under the bank, and then I saw his head quietly break the water. The dark shape of a second beaver, following him, glided like a phantom among the wavering images of the moon and trees.

I could no longer hear the barking on the hill. I was very hungry now, and intermittently felt sleepy, but here between the pond and the stream the morning air was endlessly refreshing and I entered that pleasant state of being wholly relaxed, utterly drained of muscular energy, yet suffused by awareness, interest, and approval . . . the mild, benign energies of momentary happiness.

Five or six bright yellow streamers—so they

seemed to be—approached me and sped by, dipping and rising. They were finches. The pattern of their flight was of long smooth waves, in the troughs of which they would flutter their wings to ascend the coming slope, but fold them before the top and soar curvingly over the crest. Sleek as torpedoes or little fish, they would glide downward again into the next trough and there extend their wings and flutter them.

A glossy red-winged blackbird emerged from a clump of alders and glided to a large gray stump.

Beyond the bridge the road began to climb. On both sides vigorous ferns, green but no longer the vivid green of summer, crowded the sunny space before the trees. There was a coolness of night in the woods and it poured into the road, mingling with the warmer air.

Abruptly I heard and saw him, and though no creature is more familiar to me, more likely to be taken for granted, I was thrilled to see him again, and gladdened, more than gladdened, filled for a moment with the complex happiness of our relationship that is both less than human and utterly human. Certainly I was made happy by his show of love for me. But my admiration of him is undiminished, and I felt it again, as always. He is the handsomest of dogs, muscular and large, with tufted, golden fur. The sound of his feet was audible on the hard-packed, pebble-strewn road. I leaned forward and called to him and clapped my hands, and he accelerated, arching his throat and running with more gusto. He ran with a powerful driving stride that was almost that of a greyhound, and as he neared me he drew back his lips, arched his throat still more and let out a volley of ecstatic little *yips*. This sound was so puppyish, and his ensuing behavior so utterly without dignity, so close to fawning slavishness that one might have contemned him for it, except that it was extreme, so extreme that there was no hint of fawning, and certainly not of cringing, but the very opposite: great confidence and security, into which there rose up an ecstacy he could not contain and could not express rapidly enough to diminish, so that for a while he seemed actually to be in pain. I had to help him, had to let him lick my face protractedly and press his paws into my shoulders. And as sometimes happens in such early morning solitudes, there came over me a sense of the briefness of life, and of my kinship with all these other creatures who would soon be dead, and I almost spoke aloud to my dog: how much it matters to be alive together! how marvelous and brief our lives are! and how good it is, dear one that you are, to have the wonderful strange passion of your spirit in my life!

As he wound around me and pressed his body against mine, I remembered another greeting when I had seen blood on his teeth and feet. He was three then, in his prime. I had been away for several weeks—our first parting—and he had been baffled. When I came back I had reached this very place in the road, in my car, also in summer, when I saw him hurtling toward me. His first sounds were pathetic, a mixed barking, whimpering, and gulping for breath. I had to get out of the car to prevent him from injuring himself. I had to kneel in the road and let him kiss me and wind around me. He was weeping; I had to console him. And then he was laughing, and dancing on his hind legs, and I laughed too, except that it was then that I noticed the blood. He had been in the house, Patricia told me later, and had heard the car. He had torn open the screen door with his teeth and claws, had chewed away some protective slats and had driven his body through the opening.

He danced around me now on his hind legs, licking my face. I knew that I could terminate this ecstacy by throwing a stone for him, which I did, hard and low, so that he would not overtake it and break his teeth. A few moments later he laid it at my feet and looked into my face excitedly.

Patricia and the children were still sleeping. I ate breakfast alone, or rather, with Shawno, who waited by my chair.

I had hoped to spend the morning writing, but my eyes were closing irresistibly. I pulled up bush beans in the garden, and carried tall spikes of bolted lettuce to the compost pile. There is a rough rail fence around the garden to keep the ponies out. Shawno lay beneath it and watched me. I cleared a few weeds and from time to time got rid of stones by flinging them absently into the woods. I pulled out the brittle pea vines from their chicken wire trellis, rolled up the wire and took it to the barn. After two hours of this I went to bed. Shawno had gone in already and was enjoying a second breakfast with the children. I had forgotten about him, but as I left the garden I saw by the fence, where the grass had been flattened by his body, a little heap of stones. He had chased and brought back every one I had tried to get rid of.

•

His parents. Ida's delight. His leaping. Children in the park. An elderly scholar.

When Patricia was pregnant with Ida we were living on Riverside Drive in New York. One bright October day we saw a crowd of people at the low stone wall of the park. Many were murmuring in admiration and a few almost shouted with delight. Down below, on the grassy flat, two dogs were racing. The first belonged to an acquaintance in our building. She was tawny and short-haired with the lines of a greyhound, except for a larger head and more massive shoulders. She was in heat and was leading the other in fantastic, playful sprints, throwing her haunches against him gaily and changing direction at great speed. The male, a Belgian shepherd with golden fur, was young and in a state of transport. He ran stiff-legged, arching his neck over her body with an eagerness that seemed ruthless, except that his ears were laid back shyly. The dogs' speed was dazzling; both were beauties, and the exclamations continued as long as they remained in sight.

Shawno was the largest of the issue of those memorable nuptials. He arrived in our apartment when Ida was twelve weeks old. She looked down from her perch in Patricia's arms and saw him wobbling this way and that, and with a chortle that was almost a scream reached for him with both hands. Soon she was bawling the astonished, gasping wails of extreme alarm (his needle-point bites), and he was yelping piteously in the monkey-like grip with which she had seized his ear and was holding him at arm's length, out of mind, while she turned her tearful face to her mother.

These new beginnings, and especially my marriage with Patricia (it was my third marriage), occuring late in my maturity, ended a period of severe unhappiness. And I found that loving the child, cradling and dandling her, playing little games with her, watching her sleep, and above all watching her nurse at Patricia's breast, awakened memories of my childhood I would never have guessed were still intact. Something similar happened with the dog. I began a regimen of early morning running, as if he were an athlete and I his trainer, and I had trotted behind him through the weathers of several months before I realized that my happiness at these times was composed in part of recovered memories of the daybreak runnings of my youth, times so full of hope and satisfaction as to seem to me, now, paradisal.

The dog developed precociously. At eighteen months he was jumping seven foot walls, chasing sticks I threw for him. He was a delight to watch, powerful and beautiful, with a quality of spirit that was like the nonchalant gaiety of human youth. He became a personage in the park and acquired a band of children, who left their games to play with him, and invented new games to include him. It was not only his prowess that attracted them, but the extraordinary love he showed them. The truth was, he was simply smitten with the human race. I was crossing upper Broadway with him once; he was leashed; the crossing was crowded. There came toward us an old gentleman holding a four-year-old boy by the hand. The boy's face and the dog's were on a level, and as they passed the two faces turned to each other in mutual delight, and Shawno bestowed a kiss that began at one ear, went all the way across and ended at the other. I glanced back. The boy, too, was glancing back, grinning widely. In fact, the boy and Shawno were looking back at each other. This incident is paired for all time with another that I witnessed in New York and that perhaps could not have occurred in any other city. It was in the subway at rush hour. The corridors were booming with the grinding roar of the trains and the pounding of thousands of almost running feet. Three corridors came together in a Y and two of them were streaming with people packed far tighter than soldiers in military formation. The columns were approaching each other rapidly. There was room to pass, but just barely, or not quite. The columns collided. That is, their inside corners did, and these were occupied by apparently irascible men. Each hurled one, exactly one, furious roundhouse blow at the other, and both were swept away in their columns—a memorable fight.

I would never have known certain people in New York had it not been for the loving spirit of the dog; worse, it would never have occurred to me that knowing them was desirable, or possible, where in fact it was delightful. The people I mean were children. What could I have done with them had it not been for the dog? As it was, I changed my hours in order to meet them, and they—a group of eight or so—waited for us devotedly after school. Most were Puerto Rican. The youngest was only seven, the eldest eleven. They would spread themselves in a circle with the dog in the center and throw a ball back and forth, shouting as he leaped and tried to snatch it from the air. When he succeeded, which was often, one saw the merriest and most musical of chases, the boys arranged behind the dog according to speed of foot, the dog holding the ball high, displaying it provocatively, looking back over his shoulder and trotting stiff-legged just fast enough to elude the foremost boy, winding that laughing, shouting, almost singing line of children this way and that through the park. Invariably the boys asked me to make him leap, and I would throw the ball over fences and walls. Perhaps in emulation of the dog—and certainly because I myself wanted to do more than watch—we began a game of leaping, or rather of flying through the air, the boys diving headfirst from the steep stone wall by the stairs, holding out their arms like wings . . . and I would catch them at the armpits and set them on the ground. Most were too heavy to dive from very high, but one, a bold and wiry seven-year-old, launched himself from heights that made a few bystanders turn away in horror. He held out his arms like sparrows' wings, and lifted his head, his face shining with bliss. I would catch him and he would dart away to try it again, apparently unaware of the awe and the smiles of admiration on the faces of his friends. I discovered later that some of our audience came on purpose at this time to watch the children and the dog. One elderly, white-haired man I have never forgotten. He was Jewish and spoke with a German accent, wore a felt hat and expensive coats. He came to the playground regularly and stood with his hands behind his back, his head dropped forward, nodding and chuckling, and smiling unweariedly. His face was wonderful. It was intelligent and kindly, was still strong, still handsome, and it possessed a quality I have come to associate with genius, an apparent unity of feeling, an alacrity and wholeness of response. Whatever he was feeling suffused his face; he did not have attitudes toward his feelings, and counter-attitudes toward his attitudes. The dog delighted him. He deferred to the headlong, boisterous children, who when Shawno would appear, would shout happily and in unison, and Shawno would go to them, bounding exuberantly, but it would not be long before the old gentleman would call him, and Shawno would leave the children, not bounding now but sweeping his tail in such extreme motions that his hind legs performed a little dance from side to side independently of his front legs. The old gentleman would lean over him, speak to him and pet him, and the dog would press against his legs and look into his face. We usually talked for a few minutes before I went home. When I asked him about his work and life he waved away the questions with gestures that were humorous and pleading yet were impressive in their authority. One day I recognized his face in a photograph in the *Times*, alas, on the obituary page. He was an eminent refugee scholar, a sociologist. I discovered, reading the description of his career, that I had studied briefly with his son at Columbia. By this time we had moved to the remote farmhouse in the country and our second child had been born.

•

Past lives. Streams. An incident in the woods. Ferocity and family concern.

Our house had been occupied by Finns, as had many others near us. The hill, actually a ridge, sloped away on two sides, one forested and the other, to the south, open pasture with the remnants of an orchard. At the bottom of these fields was a stream, and in an arm of the stream, a sauna. It was here that the old Finn who had built the house had bathed his invalid wife, carrying her back and forth every day until her final illness. From this same small pool he had carried water in buckets to the garden a few strides away. The sauna was damaged beyond repair, but we let it stand; and we brought back the garden, which now was one of three. For the few years that country living sustained the glow of romance, this garden was my favorite, and I carried water to it in buckets, as had the old man. Just beyond the sauna a wooded slope rose steeply. Racoons and deer entered our field here, and it was here that the ponies and dog all came to drink.

There were other relics of those vanished lives: handmade apple boxes with leather hinges cut from old boots; door handles in all the sheds made of sapling crotches; a split round apple ladder with flakes of spruce bark on the sides and rungs made of rock maple saplings; ten foot Finnish skis that had been cut by hand and bent at the tips with steam from a kettle. There were hills wherever one looked, and there had been farms on all the hills. Some of the Finns had skied to market, and had cruised their woodlots on skis. Some of their children had skied to school.

The hills and ridges are so numerous that in the spring, while the snow is melting, the sound of water can be heard everywhere. It pours and tumbles; there is a continual roaring; and when the thaw is well advanced the large stream in the valley makes the frightening sounds of flood, hurling chunks of ice ahead of it, crowding violently into the curves, and hurtling over falls so deep in spume that the rocks cannot be seen. Later, in the hot weather, one hears the braided sounds and folded sounds of quiet water. The orange gashes and abrasions on the trunks of trees are darkening. More trees are dead. The banks of the streams, however beautiful, and however teeming with new life, are strewn with debris in many stages of decay.

The streams have become presences in my life. For a while they were passions. There are few that I haven't fished and walked to their source. These have been solitary excursions, except for the single time that I took the dog. His innocent trotting at the water's edge disturbed the trout. Still worse was his drinking and wading in the stream. I called him out. He stood on the bank and braced his legs and shook himself. Rather, he was seized by a violent shaking, a shaking so swift and powerful as to seem like a vibration. It shook his head from side to side, then letting his head come to rest seized his shoulders and shook them, then his ribs, and in a swift, continuous wave passed violently to his haunches, which it shook with especial vigor, and then entered his tail and shook the entire length of it, and at last, from the very tip, sprang free, leaving behind, at the center of the now-subsided aura of sparkling waterdrops, an invigorated and happy dog. It was at this moment of perfected well-being that one of those darting slim shadows caught his eye. He was electrified. He hurled himself into the water head first, thrusting his snout to the very bottom, where he rooted this way and that. He emerged and looked in amazement from side to side. The trout had vanished without trace. He had no notion even of the direction of its flight. He thrust down his head again and turned over stones, then came up, smooth and muscular with his streaming fur clinging to his body, and stood there peering down, poised in the electric stillness of the hunter that seems to be a waiting but is actually a fascination. Years later, after my own passion for trout had cooled, I would see him poised like that in the shallows of the swimming hole, ignoring the splashing, shouting children, looking down, still mesmerized, still ready—so he thought—to pounce.

During most of the thaw there is little point in going into the woods. Long after the fields have cleared and their brown is touched with green, there'll be pools and streaks of granular snow, not only in the low-lying places in the woods, but on shadowed slopes and behind rocks. For a while the topmost foot of soil is too watery to be called mud. The road to our house becomes impassible, and for days, or one week, or two, or three, we walk home from the store wearing rubber boots and carrying the groceries and perhaps the youngest children in knapsacks and our arms. This was once a corduroy road, and it never fails that some of the logs have risen again to the surface.

Spring in the north is almost violent. After the period of desolation, when the snow has gone and everything that once was growing seems to have been bleached and crushed, and the soil itself seems to have been killed by winter, there comes, accompanied by the roaring of the streams, a prickling of the tree buds that had formed in the cold, and a prickling of little stems on the forest floor, and a tentative, small stirring of bird life. This vitalizing process, once begun, becomes bolder, more lavish, and larger, and soon there is green everywhere, and the open fretwork of branches, limbs, and trunks, beyond which, all winter, we had seen sky, hills, and snow, has become an eye-stopping mass of green. The roaring of the streams diminishes, but the velocity of green increases until the interlocking leaves cannot claim another inch of sunlight except by slow adjustment and the killing of rival growth. Now the animal presence is spread widely through the woods, and Shawno runs this way and that, nose to the ground, so provoked by scents that he cannot concentrate and remains excited and distracted by overlapping trails.

It was in this season of early summer that we came here. The woods were new to me. I was prepared for wonders. And there occurred a small but strange encounter that did indeed prove haunting. We had been walking a woods road, Shawno and I, or the ghost of a road, and came to a little dell, dense with ferns and the huge leaves of young striped maples. Shawno drew close to me and seem disturbed. He stood still for a moment sniffing the air instead of the ground and then the fur rose on his neck and he began to growl. At that moment there emerged from the semi-dark of a dense leaf bank perhaps thirty steps away, two dogs, who stopped silently and came no further. The smaller dog was a beagle, the larger a German shepherd, black and gigantic. His jowls on both sides and his snout in front bristled with white-shafted porcupine quills. He did not seem to be in pain, but seemed helpless and pathetic, a creature without fingers or tools, and therefore doomed. The uncanny thing about the dogs was their stillness. That intelligence, that seems almost human and that in their case was amplified by the cooperative rationality of their companionship, was refusing contact of any sort not only with me but with the dog at my side. Shawno continued to growl and to stamp his feet uncertainly. Just as silently as they had appeared, the beagle and the shepherd turned into the undergrowth and vanished.

I was to see these two dogs again. In the meantime, I learned that it was not uncommon for dogs to run wild, or to lead double lives; and that such pairings of scent and sight were frequent. The beagle could follow a trail. The shepherd had sharp eyes, was strong and could kill.

In the city there had been but one threat to Shawno's life. Here there were several. He was large and tawny, and though he was lighter in color than a deer, he resembled a deer far more closely than had the cows, sheep, and horses which in the memory of my neighbors had been shot for deer—certainly more closely than had the goat that had been gutted in the field and brought to the village on the hood of the hunter's car. With such anecdotes in mind, I discovered one day, toward the end of hunting season, that Shawno had escaped from the house. At least eight hunters had gone up our road into the woods. I know now that his life was not at quite the risk that I imagined, but at that time I was disturbed. I ran into the woods calling to him and whistling, praying for his survival and wondering how I should find him if, already, he had been shot. Several hours later, his courting finished (probably it had been that) he emerged into our field loping and panting, and came into the house, and with a clatter of elbows and a thump of his torso dropped into his nook by the woodstove. He held his head erect and looked at me. The corners of his lips were lifted. His mouth was open to the full, and his extended tongue, red with exertion, vibrated with his panting in a long, highly arched curve that turned up again at its tip. He blinked as the warmth took hold of him, and with a grunt that was partly a sigh stretched his neck forward and dropped his chin on his paws.

In February of that winter I saw the beagle and German shepherd again. We were sharing a load of hay with a distant neighbor, an elderly man whose bachelor brother had died and who was living alone among the bleached and crumbling remains of what had been once a considerable farm. He still raised a few horses and trained them for harness, though there wasn't a living in it. I had backed the truck into the barn and was tossing up bales to him where he stood in the hayloft when a car drew up and a uniformed man got out. I recognized the game warden, though I had never met him. He was strikingly different from the police of the county seat ten miles away, who walked with waddling gaits and could be found at all hours consuming ice cream at the restaurant on the highway south. The warden was large but trim, was actually an imposing figure, as he needed to be—he had made enemies, and they had tried to kill him, once by shooting through the window, another time by throwing a gasoline bomb that had brought down the house in flames, at night, in winter. He and his wife and adolescent son had escaped. He was spoken of as a fanatic, but hunters praised his skill as a hunter. A man who had paid a fine for poaching said to me, "If he's after you in the woods he'll git you. No man can run through the woods like him." His large round eyes were a pale blue. Their gaze was unblinking, open, disturbingly strange.

He addressed the elderly man by his last name. The warden, too, was a scion of an old, old family here.

"We'd all be better off," he said, "if you'd kept him chained."

His voice was emphatic but not angry. He spoke with the unconscious energy and loudness that one hears in many of the rural voices. "He's been runnin' deer, and you know it. I caught him at the carcass. It was still kickin'." The warden handed him the piece of paper he had been carrying, which was obviously a summons. "I've done away with him," he said.

28

We had come out of the barn. The warden opened the trunk of his car and brought out the small stiff body of the beagle. Its eyes and mouth were open, its tongue protruded between its teeth on one side, and its chest was matted with blood. The warden laid the body on the snowbank by the barn and said, "Come back to the car a minute."

The black German shepherd lay on a burlap sack, taking up the whole of the trunk.

"You know who owns that?"

The elderly man shook his head. No emotion had appeared on his face since the warden had arrived. The warden turned his blue, strangely unaggressive eyes on me and repeated the question. I too shook my head. The shepherd had been home since I had seen him in the woods: someone had pulled out the quills.

Shawno was barking from the cab of the truck. I had left the window open to give him air. It was his questioning, information-wanting bark. The smell of the dead dogs had reached him.

After the warden left, my neighbor went into the house and came back with money for the hay.

"Obliged to you for haulin' it," he said, and that was all.

That night, on the phone, I told a friend, a hunter, about the dogs.

"The warden was right," he said. "Dogs like that can kill a deer a day, even more. Jake Wesley's dogs cornered a doe in my back field last year. She was pregnant with twins. They didn't bother killing her, they don't know how, they were eating her while she stood there. She was ripped to shreds. I shot them both."

There was a crust on the snow just then. Dogs could run on it, but the sharp hooves of the deer would break through and the ice cut their legs. They spent such winters herded in evergreen groves, or "yards," and if the bark and buds gave out many would starve. Occasionally the wardens took them hay, but this introduced another problem, for if the dogs found the snowmobile trails and followed them to the yards, the slaughter could be severe.

And what of Shawno? I realized that I regarded him habitually with the egocentricity of a doting master, as if he were a creature chiefly of his human relations, though certainly I knew better. I thought of the many cats his ferocious mother had killed. And I remembered how, the previous fall, while our children were playing with a neighbor's children in front of our house, Shawno had come into their midst with a freshly killed woodchuck. He held his head high and trotted proudly among us, displaying his kill. It was a beautiful chestnut color and it dangled flexibly full-length from his teeth, jouncing limply as he trotted. He placed it on the ground under the large maple, where he often lay, and stretched out regally above it, lion-like, the corpse between his paws. I was tying a shoelace for one of the children. I heard a rushing growl of savagery and out of the corner of my eye saw Shawno spring forward. I shouted and jumped in front of him. One of the visiting boys had come too close.

I doubt that Shawno would have bitten him. Nevertheless, in that frightening moment I had seen and heard the animal nervous system that is not like ours, but is capable of an explosive violence we never approximate, even in our most excessive rages.

He was with me in the pickup one day when I went for milk to a neighbor's dairy. There were usually dogs in front of the barn and Shawno was on friendly terms with them. This time, however, before I had shut the motor, he leaped across me in the cab, growling and glaring, his snout wrinkled and his front teeth bared to the full. His body was tense, and instantaneously had been charged with an extraordinary energy. Down below, also growling, was a large black hound with yellow eyes. The window was open. Before I could close it or speak to him, Shawno put his head and shoulders through the opening, and with a push of his hind feet that gouged the seat cover, dove down on the hound.

There were no preliminaries. They crashed together with gnashing teeth and a savage, high-pitched screaming.

The fight was over in a moment. Shawno seized him by the neck, his upper teeth near the ear, his lower on the throat, and driving forward with his powerful hind legs twisted him violently to the ground.

The hound tried to right himself. Shawno responded with siren-like growls of rage and a munching and tightening of teeth that must have been excruciating. The hound's yellow eyes flashed. He ceased struggling. Shawno growled again, and this time shook his head from side to side in the worrying motion with which small animals are killed. The hound lay still. Shawno let him up. The hound turned its head away. Shawno pressed against him, at right angles, extending his chin and entire neck over the hound's shoulder. The hound turned its head as far as it could in the other direction.

The fight was over. There was no battle for survival, as in the Jack London stories that had thrilled me in my youth. Survival lay precisely not in tooth and claw, but in the social signalling that tempered the dogs' savagery, as it tempered that of wolves. It was this that accounted for the fact that one never came upon the carcasses of belligerent dogs who had misconceived their powers, as had the hound.

The victory was exhilarating. What right had I, who had done nothing but watch, to feel exultation and pride? Yet I did feel these things. Shawno felt them too, I am sure. He sat erect beside me going home, and there was still a charge of energy, an aura about his body. He held his head proudly, or so I thought. His mouth was open, his tongue lolled forward and he was panting lightly. From time to time he glanced aside at me out of narrowed eyes. I kept looking at him, kept smiling and couldn't stop. I reached across and stroked his head and spoke to him, and again he would glance at me. He was like the roughneck athlete heroes of my youth, who after great feats in the sandlot or high school football games, begrimed, bruised, and wet-haired, would walk to the locker rooms or the cars, heads high, helmets dangling from their fingertips or held in the crooks of their arms, riding sweet tides of exhaustion and praise. I remembered the glorious occasions, too, after I had come of an age to compete, when my brief inspirations on the field had been rewarded by teammates' arms around my shoulders.

But there was more to it than this. It was as if I had been made larger and stronger by his power; it was as if my very existence had been multiplied because he was my ally and loved me. These, so I take it, were the feelings of the boy who still lived within me and who looked with happy gratitude at this guardian with thick fur and fearsome teeth, who could leap nonchalantly over the truck we now rode in, and who had devoted his powers utterly to the boy's well-being.

Very little of this came into my voice when I said at home, "Shawno got into a fight!"

Ida and Patricia came close to me, asking, "What happened? What happened?"

Ida had never witnessed the animal temper I have just described. What she wanted to know was, had he been bitten?

If anyone had said to Shawno what the little boy says in Ida's *Mother Goose*—"Bow wow wow, whose dog art thou?" he could not have answered except by linking Ida's name with my own. He often sat by her chair when she ate. Three of the five things he knew to search for and fetch belonged to Ida: her shoes, her boots, her doll. When I read to her in the evening she leaned against me on the sofa and Shawno lay on the other side with his head in her lap. Often she fell asleep while I read, and we would leave her there until we ourselves were ready for bed. When we came for her Shawno would be asleep beside her. On the nights when I carried her, still awake, to her bed, she would insist that both Shawno and Patricia come kiss her goodnight, and both would. Usually he would leap into the bed, curl up beside her and spend part of the night. When she was five or six we bought two shaggy ponies from a neighbor and having fenced the garden let them roam as they would. The larger pony had been gelded, but was still mischievous and inclined to nip. Late one afternoon I glanced from an upstairs window and saw Ida leading Liza and Jacob across the yard, all three holding hands. Jacob had just learned to walk and they were going slowly. The ponies came behind them silently. Starbright, the gelding, drew close to Jacob and seemed about to nudge him, which he had done several times in recent weeks, toppling him over. Shawno was watching from across the yard. He sprang forward and came running in a crouch, close to the ground. I called Patricia to the window. His style was wonderful to see, so calm and masterly. There had been a time when he had harried the ponies gleefully, chasing them up and down the road without mercy, snapping at their feet, leaping at their shoulders, and dodging their kicks with what, to them, must have been exasperating ease. I had had to reprimand him several times before he would give it up. Now silently, and crouching menacingly he moved in behind the children and turned to face the ponies. Starbright knew that he would leap but did not know when, and began to lift his feet apprehensively. Shawno waited . . . and waited . . . and the pony apparently breathed a sigh of relief, and abruptly Shawno leapt, darting like a snake at Starbright's feet. The pony pulled back in alarm, and wheeled, obliging the smaller pony to wheel too. Shawno let them come along then, but followed the children himself, glancing back to see that the ponies kept their distance. The children hadn't seen a bit of this. "What a darling!" said Patricia. "What a dear dog!"

•

Down to Searles.

The owners of bitches, when their dogs were in heat, were often obliged to call the owners of males and request that they be taken home and chained. Four days went by once before we could locate Shawno. At last the call came. He had traveled several miles. When I went for him he wouldn't obey me, was glassy-eyed and frantic. The only way to get him home was to put the bitch in the car and lure him. It was pathetic. He hadn't slept for four days, was thin, had been fighting with other males, and had had no enjoyment at all: the bitch was a feisty little dachshund. For two days he lay chained on the porch lost utterly in gloom. He didn't respond to anyone, not even to Ida, but kept his chin flat between his paws and averted his eyes. He had gone to bitches before, but I had been able to fetch him. He had suffered frustration before, but had recovered quickly. What was different this time? I never knew.

Apart from these vigils of instinct, his absences were on account of human loves, the first and most protracted of which was not a single person but a place and situation irresistible to his nature. This was the general store.

The one-story white clapboard building was near the same broad stream that ran through the whole of the valley. The banks were steep here and the stream curved sharply, passing under a bridge and frothing noisily over a double ledge of rounded rocks. There had used to be horseshoe pits by the road and games before supper and at night under the single light at the corner of the store. Three roads converged here. One was steep and on winter Sundays and occasional evenings had been used for sledding. That was when the roads had been packed, not plowed, and the only traffic had been teams and sleds. Searles's father—the second of the three generations of C. W. Searles—

though he was known to be a hard and somewhat grasping man, would open the store and perhaps bring up cider for the sledders. There would be a bonfire in the road, and as many as a hundred people in motion around it.

Searles was sixty years old when we arrived. The store was wonderfully well organized and good to look at, crowded but neat and logical, filled with implements of the local trades and pleasures. Searles had worked indoors for his father as a boy. Later as a youth, he had gone with a cart and horse to the outlying farms, taking meat, hardware, clothing, and tools and bringing back not cash but eggs, butter, apples, pears, chickens, shingles. Now when he ordered the paté called *creton*, he knew it would be consumed by the Dulacs, Dubords, and Pelletiers. The five sets of rubber children's boots were for the Sawyers and were in the proper sizes. He displayed them temptingly, brought down the price, and finally said, "Why don't you take the lot, Charlie, and make me an offer?" He knew who hunted and who fished, and what state their boots, pants, and coats were in. A death in the town affected his business. He saw the price of bullets going sky-high, put in several shell- and bullet-making kits, and said, "Verne, what do you figure you spend a year on shells and bullets?" "Oh, it's horrible. I don't practice no more, that's what's come to . . ."

In the summer there were rakes, hoes, spades, cultivators, coils of garden hose, sections of low white fencing to put around flower beds, and perhaps a wheelbarrow arrayed on the loading apron in front of the store. In the fall, on the same apron, one found crated wood stoves, sections of black stove pipe, rolls of asphalt sheeting, rolls of plastic sheeting for window insulation, while inside, on racks, were checkered red and black hunting coats of thick wool, orange vests, orange caps, boxes of shells. When the getting-ready time was past and winter was really here, one saw stacks of broad shovels out front, and two or three of the large, flat-bottomed snow scoops that had to be pushed with both hands. Set up in rows on the window shelves were insulated rubber boots with felt liners, and two styles of snowshoes, glistening with varnish. Late in winter the sugaring supplies appeared: felt filters, wooden and metal spiggots, zinc buckets with creased lids; and these were followed shortly by the racks of seeds to be started indoors, and the new fishing rods, new reels, the same old lures and hooks. At all times there were axes and axe handles, bucksaws, wooden wedges and iron wedges, birch hooks, a peavey or two, many chainsaw files and cans of oil. For years he kept a huge skillet that finally replaced, as he knew it would, the warped implement at the boys' camp. He carried kitchenware and electrical and plumbing supplies, and tools for carpentry, as well as drugstore items, including a great deal of Maalox. All this was in addition to the food, the candy rack, the newspapers, the greeting cards, and the school supplies.

People stopped to talk. Those he liked—some of whom he had sat beside in the little red schoolhouse up the road, long unused now—would stand near the counter for half an hour exchanging news or pleasantries. One day I heard Franklin Mason, who was five years older than Searles, say testily, "I seen 'em, I seen 'em." He was referring to the shingling brackets that had been propped up prominently at the end of the counter. Searles had known for two years that Mason wanted to replace his roofing; he had just learned that Mason had decided on asphalt shingles. "I might borrow Mark's brackets," said Mason, but he added, in a different tone, scratching his face, "these are nice, though . . ."

People didn't say "Searles's place," but "down to Searles." "Oh, they'll have it down to Searles." "I stopped in down to Searles." "Let me just call down to Searles." He was C. W. the third, but had been called Bob all his life.

Of the men in the village he was certainly the least rural. He had grown up on a farm, loved to hunt and fish, play poker, drink whisky, and swap yarns. But he had gone away to college, and then to business school, and had worked in Boston for three years. He was not just clever or smart but was extremely intelligent, with a meticulous, lively, retentive mind. He had come home not because he couldn't make a go of things in the city, but because he loved the village and the countryside and sorely missed the people. He subscribed to *The Wall Street Journal* and *The New York*

Times, read many periodicals, was interested in politics and controversy and changing customs. When I met him his three children were away at college. We disagreed irreconcilably on politics. I was aware of his forbearance and was grateful for it. And I was impressed by his wit, and by his kindliness, as when, without reproach or impatience he would allow certain impoverished children to cluster for long, long minutes before the candy rack, blocking his narrow aisle; and as when he built a ramp for the wheelchair of a neighbor who could no longer walk but was still alert and lively. He was not a happy man. He drank too much to be healthy, and his powers of mind by and large went unused. Yet one could sense in him a bedrock of contentment, and a correct choice of place and work. He was tall and bony, carried far too large a stomach, and was lame in one leg. In damp weather he used a cane and moved with some difficulty about the store. I came to see that most of his friends were old friends and were devoted to him. I learned too that he had forgiven many debts and had signed over choice lots of land to the town, one for a ball field, another for picnics. His gregarious cocker spaniel, who possessed no territorial sense at all, lounged in the aisles and corners, and on sunny days could be found on the loading apron under the awning. And it was here, in front of the store, beside the caramel colored spaniel, that one sunny day I encountered my own dog, who had vanished from the house.

He leaped up gaily, showing no guilt at all, and came beside me when I went into the store.

Searles, on the high stool, was leaning over the *Wall Street Journal* that was spread across the counter. The moment he raised his head, Shawno looked at him alertly.

Searles smiled at me. "I've got a new friend," he said; and to the dog, "Haven't I, Shawno? What'll you have, Shawno? Do you want a biscuit? Do you?" Shawno reared, put his front paws on the counter and barked.

"Oh you do?" said Searles. "Well I happen to have one."

He put his hand under the counter, where he kept the dog biscuits that had fattened the spaniel.

"Will you pay for it now?" he said. "Will you? Will you, Shawno?"

Shawno, whose paws were still on the counter, barked in a deep, almost indignant way. Searles was holding the biscuit, not offering it.

"Oh you want it on credit?" he said. He held up the biscuit, and at the sight of it the dog barked in lighter, more eager tones. "What?" said Searles, "You want it free?" Again Shawno barked, the eagerness mixed now with impatience and demand. "All right," said Searles, "Here 'tis. On the house." He held it out and Shawno took it with a deft thrust of his head.

I had watched all this with a long-lasting, not-quite-fitting smile.

I said that I hoped the dog wasn't a nuisance.

"Oh no," said Searles, "He's a good dog. He's a fine dog."

And I looked at Shawno, who was looking at Searles, and I thought, "You wretch, you unfaithful wretch! How easy it is to buy you!"

Yet I let him go back there again and again. He'd trot away in the morning as if he were going off to work, and then at suppertime would appear on the brow of the hill, muddied and wet, having jumped into the stream to drink.

I didn't have the heart to chain him. And I couldn't blame him. What better place for a gregarious dog than this one surviving social fragment of the bygone town? There were other dogs to run with, there was the store itself with its pleasant odors, there was Searles, my rival, with his biscuits, there were children to make much of him, and grown-ups by the score. Moreover, there were cars, trucks, and delivery vans, and all had been marked by the dogs of distant places. We would arrive for groceries or mail and find him stretched on the apron in front of the store, or playing in the road with other dogs, or standing in a cluster of kids with bikes, or stationed by the counter inside, looking up inquiringly at customers who were chatting with Searles.

My jealousy grew. I was disgruntled and seriously ill-at-ease. Somewhere within me I was saying, "Don't you love me anymore? Have you forgotten how I raised you and trained you? Have you forgotten those mornings in the park when I threw sticks for you and taught you to leap? Have you forgotten our walks here in the woods, and the thousand discoveries we've made together?"

Most serious of all was his absence while I worked. I had built a little cabin half a mile from the house. He had been a presence, almost a tutelary spirit, in the very building of it, and then he had walked beside me every day to and from it, and had lain near my feet while I wrote or read. Often when I turned to him he would already have seen the movement and I would find his eyes waiting for mine.

Those inactive hours were a poor substitute for the attractions of the store, and I knew it, in spite of our companionable lunches and afternoon walks. But what of me?

One day, several weeks after his first visit to the store, I jumped into the car and went down there rather speedily, ordered him rather firmly into the back seat, and took him home. I did the same thing the following day. The day after that I chained him, and the day after that chained him again . . .

Life returned to normal. I took away the chain. He was grateful and stopped moping. I saw that he had renounced his friends at the store, and I was glad, forgetting that I had forced him to do it. Anyway, those diversions had never cancelled his love for me—so I reminded myself, and began to see fidelity where I had established dependence. But that didn't matter. The undiminished, familiar love wiped out everything—at least for me.

•

Eddie Dubord.
Sawyer's Labrador.
Quills.

Just below us in the woods the stream was speeded by a short channel of granite blocks, though the mill wheel was gone that once had turned continuously during thaw, reducing small hills of cedar drums to stacks of shingles. There had been trout for a while in the millrace, but chubs, that eat the eggs of trout, had driven them away.

Upstream of this ghost of a mill, just beyond the second of two handsome waterfalls, one stringer of a rotted bridge still joined the banks. Snowmobilers had dropped a tree beside it and had nailed enough crossboards to make a narrow path. I had crossed it often on showshoes, and then on skis, and the dog had trotted behind, but there came a day in spring, after the mud had dried, that Shawno drew back and stood there on the bank stamping his feet, moving from side to side indecisively, and barking. He had seen the turbulent water between the boards of the bridge. I picked him up and carried him across, and couldn't help laughing, he was so big, such a complicated bundle in my arms, and I remembered how he had nestled there snugly as a pup, lighter and softer than Ida.

Beyond the bridge a grassy road curved away into the trees. In somewhat more than a mile it would join the tarred road, but halfway there, on the inside of its curve, a wagon trail branched off, now partly closed by saplings. It was here at the corner of this spur that my neighbor, Eddie Dubord, built a small cabin similar to my own.

It was summer. The dog had gone with the children to the swimming hole and I was walking alone carrying a small rod and a tin of worms. I saw two wedges of smoke ahead of me, expanding and thinning in the slight breeze, and then I saw a parked car and a man working at something. The smoke was blowing toward him and came from two small fires spaced twelve feet apart. The man was blocky and short. He wore a visored cap of bright orange and a chore jacket of dark blue denim. His movements were stiff and slow, yet there was something impressive and attractive about the way he worked. Every motion achieved something and led to the next without waste or repetition. He went to one of the fires carrying an axe, which he used only to lift some pine boughs from a pile. He threw several on each of the fires. I walked closer, but stopped again and watched him. We had never met, but I knew that it was Dubord. He was seventy-four years old. He had driven the corner stakes to mark the floor of a cabin, had tied a cord on one of them and had carried it around the others.

Apparently he had already levelled the cord. I watched him as he picked up a five-foot iron bar and went away dragging a stoneboat that was simply the hood of an ancient car turned upside down and fitted with a rope that could be used as a yoke. He stopped at a pile of stones, and with his bar levered a large flat stone onto the car hood. With the same bar he lifted the yoke to where he could reach it. He stepped into the yoke, placed it across his chest and under his armpits, and angling his substantial weight sharply forward, using the heavy bar now as a staff, set the skid in motion and dragged it easily to one of the corner stakes. When I walked by he was on his hands and knees firming the stone and didn't see me.

Several days later I went that way again, and again stopped to watch him. He had finished the floor and had built a low platform the length of it, and had equipped the platform with steps. He would be able to work on the rafters and roof without resorting to a ladder.

He had assembled several units of studs, rafters, and cross braces, and now as I watched he pushed one erect with a stick, and caught it in the fork of a long pole that held it while he adjusted it for plumb. He nailed bracing boards at the sides, and drove in permanent nails at the base. His concentration was remarkable. It was as total and self-forgetful as a child's. Later, after I had come to know him well, I marvelled more, not less, at this quality. I had seen him at work on all kinds of things: radios and TVs, pop-up toasters, lawn mowers, snowblowers, Rototillers, outboard motors, locks, shotguns, clocks. On several occasions I had come close to him and had stood beside him wondering how to announce my presence . . . but it had never mattered how—he had looked up always with a start of panic, and then had blushed. It was not merely as if his concentration had been disturbed, but as if some deep, continuous melody had been shattered. Then he would smile shyly and greet me in his unassuming, yet gracious, almost courtly way.

He had already roofed the cabin and was boarding the sides—on the diagonal, as the old farmhouses were boarded—when we finally met. And as has often happened, it was the dog who introduced us, ignoring utterly the foolish shyness on both sides.

The smudge fires were going again to drive away the bugs. A small stack of rough-cut boards lay on a pallet of logs. Dubord had just hung the saw on a prong of the sawhorse and was carrying a board to the wall when Shawno trotted up to him and barked. He was startled and backed away defensively, ready to use the board as a weapon. But Shawno was wagging his tail in the extreme sweeps of great enthusiasm, and he did something he had almost abandoned since our coming to the country: he reared up, put his paws on Dubord's broad chest and tried to lick his weathered, leathery face with its smoke-haze of white stubble beard. By the time I reached them Shawno had conquered him utterly. Dubord was patting the dog, bending over him, and talking to him in that slurred, attractive baritone voice that seemed to have knurls in it, a grain and dark hue as of polished walnut, and that he seemed to savor in his throat and on his tongue, just as he savored tobacco, black coffee, and whisky. And of course he knew the dog's name, as he knew my name, and as I knew his. It was the simplest thing in the world to shake hands and be friends.

To hold Dubord's hand was like holding a leather sack filled with chunks of wood. His fingers were three times the size of ordinary fingers. He scarcely gripped my hand, but politely allowed me to hold his. Gravely he said, "Pleased to meet you," and then his small blue eyes grew lively behind the round, steel-framed spectacles. "I'd ask you in," he said, "but there ain't much difference yet between out and in. You got time for a drink?" I said I did, and he opened the toolbox and handed me a pint of Four Roses.

His skull was shaped like a cannonball. His jaw was broad and gristly. Everything about him suggested strength and endurance, yet his dominant trait, I soon came to see, was thoughtfulness. He listened, noticed, reflected, though it was apparent, even now, that these qualities must often have been overwhelmed in his youth by passions of one kind or another. He had come from Quebec at the age of twenty, and for almost two decades had worked in lumber camps as a woodcutter and cook. He had farmed here in this valley, both as a hired hand and on his own—had dug wells, built houses, barns, and sheds, had installed his own electric lines and his own plumbing, had raised animals and crops of all kinds. In middle age he had married a diminutive, high-tempered, rotund, childishly silly, childishly gracious woman. They had never had children. They had never even established a lasting peace. Her crippled mother lived with them in the small house he had built, knitting in an armchair near the TV while her daughter dusted the china knickknacks and photographs of relatives, straightened the paper flowers in their vases, and flattened the paper doilies they had placed under everything. Dubord liked all this, or rather, approved it, but felt ill at ease with his heavy boots and oil-stained pants, and spent his days in a shed beside the house. There, surrounded by his hundreds of small tools, he tinkered at the workbench or table saw, repairing things or building them, listening to cassettes of French Canadian fiddle music, and occasionally putting aside the tools to play his own fiddle. The camp in the woods served the same purposes as the shed, but promised longer interludes of peace.

I got to know him that summer and fall, but it was not until winter—our family's third in the little town—that Dubord and I realized that we were friends.

The deep snow of our first winter had made me giddy with excitement. The silence in the woods, the hilly terrain with its many streams, most of them frozen and white, but a few audible with a muted, far-off gurgling under their covering of ice and snow, occasional sightings of the large white snowshoe hares, animal tracks—all this had been a kind of enchantment and had recalled boyhood enjoyments that once had been dear to me. I went through the woods on snowshoes, and Shawno came behind. The following year I discovered the lightweight, highly arched, cross-country skis, my speed was doubled, and our outings became strenuous affairs for the dog. Often he sank to his shoulders and had to bound like a porpoise. Except in the driest, coldest snow, he stopped frequently, and pulling back his lips in a silent snarl, bit away the snow impacted between his toes. His tawny, snow-cleaned, winter-thickened fur looked handsome against the whiteness. When we came to downhill stretches I would speed ahead, and he would rally and follow at a run.

We had taken a turn like this through the woods in our third year, on a sunny, blue-skied day in March, when I decided to visit Dubord.

I could smell the smoke of his tin chimney before I could see it. Then the cabin came in view. His intricately webbed, gracefully curved snowshoes leaned against the depleted stack of firewood that early in the winter had filled the overhang of the entranceway.

I could hear music. It was the almost martial, furiously rhythmic music of the old country dances . . . but there seemed to be two fiddles.

Shawno barked and raced ahead . . . and Dubord's pet red squirrel bounded up the woodpile. When I reached the camp, Shawno was dancing on his hind legs barking angrily and complainingly, and the healthy, bright-eyed squirrel was crouching in a phoebe's nest under the roof, looking down with maddening calm. The music stopped, the door opened, and Dubord greeted us cheerfully—actually with a *merry* look on his face.

"You won't get that old squirrel, Shawno," he said. "He's too fast for you. You'll never get 'im. Might's well bark . . ."

"Come in," he said. "I just made coffee. Haven't seen those for a while. Where'd you get 'em?"

He meant the skis. He had never seen a manufactured pair, though he had seen many of the eight- and nine-foot handmade skis the Finns had used. He didn't know why (he said later) only the Finns had used them. Everyone else had stayed with snowshoes, which were an Indian invention.

"Nilo Ansden used to take his eggs down to Searles on skis," he said. The Searles he meant was Bob Searles's father. "He took a shortcut one day down that hill 'cross from your place. We had a two-foot storm all night and the day before. He got halfway down and remembered Esther Barden's chicken coop was in the way, but he thought *there's enough snow to get up on the roof* . . . and there was. Once he was up there there was nothin' to do but jump, so he jumped. Had a packbasket of eggs on's back. Didn't break a one."

In the whole of any winter there are never more than a few such sunny days, gloriously sunny and blue. One becomes starved for the sun.

He left the door open and we turned our chairs to face the snow and blue sky and the vast expanse of evergreen and hardwood forest. He stirred the coals in the wood stove, opened the draft and threw in some split chunks of rock maple. There was a delicious swirling all around us of hot dry currents from the stove and cool, moist currents from the snow and woods. Occasionally a tang of wood smoke came in with the cold air.

As for the fiddle music—"Oh, I was scratchin' away," he said. "I have a lot of fiddle music on the cassettes. I put it on and play along."

His cassette recorder stood on the broad work table by the window. The violin lay beside it amidst a clutter of tools and TV parts.

"If I hear somebody's got somethin' special or new, I go over an' put it on the recorder. Take a good while to play the ones I got now. You like that fiddle music, Shawno?"—and to me: "That was a schottische you heard comin' in."

He was fond of the dog. He looked at him again and again, and there began a friendship between them that pleased me and that I never cared to interrupt.

Shawno lay on the floor twisting his head this way and that and snapping at a large glossy fly that buzzed around him. He caught it, cracked it with his teeth, and ejected it with a wrinkling of the nose. Eddie laughed and said, "That's right, Shawno, you catch that old bastard fly." The dog got up and went to him and Eddie gave him a piece of the "rat cheese" we had been eating with our coffee. For a long time Shawno sat beside him, resting his head on Eddie's knee.

We laced our coffee with Four Roses whisky and had second cups. The squirrel looked in at the window, crouching eagerly, its forepaws lifted and tucked in at the wrists, and its feathery long tail arched forward like a canopy over its head.

"I built that platform to feed the birds, but he took over, so I let him have it. That's where the birds eat now."

He pointed to a wooden contraption hanging by a wire from a tree out front. Several chickadees fluttered around it angrily. It was rocking from the weight of the blue jay perched on its edge, a brilliant, unbelievable blue in the sunlight.

Eddie had hinged a tiny window in one of the panels of the side window. He opened it now and laid his hand on the feeding platform, a few peanuts and sunflower seeds on the palm. The squirrel shied away, but came back immediately and proceeded to eat from Eddie's hand, picking up one seed at a time. Shawno went over and barked, and the squirrel snatched up one last morsel and leaped into the eaves. Dubord closed the window, chuckling, and again the dog sat with him, this time stretched at his feet with his chin extended over one wide rubber boot.

I saw his packbasket in the corner. He used it daily to bring in water and whisky and a few tools. The handle of his axe protruded from the basket.

The basket was of ash strips, such as the Indians

make. I had bought several two towns away. Dubord had made this one himself.

"The Indians can take brown ash wherever they find it," he said. "Did you know that? They used to camp every summer on the Folsom place. Diamond National owns it now. There's brown ash down there, downhill goin' toward the pond. I used to trap beaver with one o' the men, and he showed me."

The basket was thirty years old.

He sipped his coffee.

"Have you met Mister Mouse?" he said.

"Who?"

"Don't know if he'll come while Shawno's here."

Smiling like a little boy, he said, "Keep your eyes open, but don't move. Don't even blink. He can see it."

He put a peanut on the two-by-four at the upper edge of the far wall, stepped back from it and stood there making a strange little whimpering sound. Shawno perked up his ears and became excited, but I whispered to him, *no, no . . . stay.*

Again Dubord made the squeaking sound, sucking air through his lips. Presently, quite soundlessly, a round-eared gray mouse appeared on the ledge, sniffing. It crept forward a few inches and froze, sniffing alertly and angling the delicate long antennae of its whiskers this way and that. It nibbled the peanut rapidly, listening while it ate, its bulging black eyes glinting with light from the windows and the door.

Shawno got to his feet . . . and that huge movement and the sound of his claws on the floor put an end to the performance.

Dubord came back chuckling, and stroked the dog's head.

We stayed for two hours. He talked of his early days in the States, and his years in the woods. I could hear the French Canadian and the Yankee accents alternating in his speech, the one stressing the final syllables, the other drawling them. Shawno sat close to him, sometimes upright with his chin on his knee, sometimes lying flat with his nose near the broad booted foot. Until now all his friendships had been friendships of play. This was a friendship of peace. It was one of those rare occasions on which, perhaps only momentarily, a little family of the spirit is formed.

It was good sapping weather. The days were sunny, the snow melting, the nights cold. When we saw Dubord several days later he was gathering sap from the huge maples near his camp.

A rapidly moving cloud of light gray smoke rolled over and over in the lower branches of the trees. I skied closer and saw that it was not coming from the cabin, as I had feared, nor was it smoke, but steam from a bubbling large tray of maple sap.

He had shovelled away some snow and had built a fireplace of fieldstones he had gathered in the fall. The sides were lined with scraps of metal. The back had been cut from a sheetmetal stove and was equipped with a metal chimney five feet high. A shal-

55

low tray, two feet by four, rested on top of the field-stone walls. It was from this tray that the clouds of steam were rising.

While I was examining all this Dubord came in sight, plodding blockily on snowshoes, pulling a toboggan that I recognized, since I had helped at all stages in the making of it, first splitting out boards from a squared-off log of ash, then boiling the tips, and finally nailing them around a log to cool and set. On the toboggan were two five-gallon white plastic jugs, each half-filled with sap. A tin funnel bounced against one of them, secured by a wire to its handle.

He glanced at me in a furious and bitter way. I didn't inquire what the trouble was, but took it for granted that he had been quarreling with Nellie. His teeth were clamped and his mouth was pulled down. How long he would have maintained this furious silence I don't know, but it was more than he could do to hold out against the dog. A deep blush suffused his weathered round face. He dropped the toboggan rope, and smiling helplessly bowed his head to the uprearing dog, petting him with both hands and allowing his face to be licked.

He took off the snowshoes and put more wood on the fire. The four-foot strips of white birch—*edgings* from the turning mill—had been stacked in the fall and covered with boards and scraps of asphalt roofing. Papery white bark still clung to them. The wood was well dried and burned hot—the "biscuit wood" of the old farmhouse kitchens.

The tray was slanted toward one of its forward corners, and there, with his brazing torch, Dubord had attached a little spigot. He drained some syrup into a large spoon, blew on it, and tested it with his finger.

I poured one of the jugs of new sap into the noisily bubbling syrup. The steam was sweet and had a pleasant odor.

Several galvanized buckets stood by the fire and Eddie divided the rest of the sap between two of them. I noticed that just as he had not filled the plastic jugs he did not fill the buckets—an old man's foresight, avoiding loads that might injure him.

I went with him back to the maple trees, and at last he broke his silence.

" 'Twas a damn good farm fifty years ago," he said. "I wanted to buy it but I couldn't meet the price."

The huge, slowly dying maples lined the road. There were smaller trees around them, some in the road itself, but the maples, in season, were leafy, and were well exposed to the sun, and their sap was far richer than that of forest maples. The boiling ratio would be forty to one, or even better.

Buckets, four to a tree, clung to the stout, coarse-barked trunks waist high, as if suspended from a single belt. They hung from short spouts of galvanized metal that had been driven into the tree, and were covered with metal lids that were creased in the middle and looked like roofs.

Since I was helping, we filled the jugs, and soon had sledded sixty gallons to the fire.

Nellie's canary had been killed that morning. The quarrel had followed its death.

She had been cleaning its cage and had let it out to stretch its wings.

"She could've put it in the other cage," he said.

He was stirring the boiling sap with a stick of wood, and in his anger he splashed it again and again.

" 'Twas right there under the bed," he said. "Damn thing shittin' all over the place! If I come in with one speck o' mud on my boots she raises hell! I wanted to go out. 'Don't open the door!' 'Well put 'im in the cage!' "

He thumped the tray as if he meant to drive holes through it.

"Freddie Latham was outside fillin' the oil tank," he said. "Nellie's mother'd knitted some mittens for the new baby, so Nellie says to me over her shoulder, 'Git Buddy,' and she comes right past me and opens the door. 'Yoo hoo, Freddie.' "

He ground his teeth a while.

"Git the bird!" he muttered explosively. "What'd she expect me t'do, fly up an' catch it? Damn thing flew out the door right behind her and she didn't even notice. She opened the porch door and it flew out that one too. Damn! If I had a stick o' wood in my hand I'd heaved it at 'er! You could o' heard her down t'village. 'Save Buddy! Here, Buddy! Git Buddy!' "

Dubord glared at me. "Damn thing perched on the roof o' the shed," he said, "I got some birdseed in my hand and got the ladder and started up. Freddie hauled out my smeltin' net and tried t'hand it to me. Fat lot o' good that did! Soon as Buddy saw me gittin' close he flew over an' perched on the ridgepole o' the house. Then he flew up to the antenna, and Nellie's whistlin' to him an' suckin' her lips. 'Eddie, git that canary record, maybe if we play it Buddy'll come down.' Now ain't that a goddam smart idea! If he could hear it up there what'd he want t'come down for?

"By the time I come off the ladder the bird'd flew up to the electric wire. He was just gittin' settled . . . wham! Some damn ol' red-tail hawk been watchin' the whole thing. I never seen 'im. Where he come from I don't know. Couple o' yella feathers come down like snowflakes. I thought, here's your canary, Nellie. An' I thought, enjoy your dinner, mister hawk. You just saved me two hund'd dolluhs."

Eddie faced me and stood absolutely still. "Yessuh!" he said. "That's what I said! Two hund'd dolluhs! That's what I spent for birdseed! I'm tellin' the truth, I ain't makin' it up! And I ain't sayin' Buddy et that much, I'm saying we BOUGHT that much! You seen him do that Christly trick! You and the Missus seen that trick the first time you come down. Sure you did! You had the girl with you . . ."

The trick he was referring to was something Nellie had taught the bird, or had discovered, namely, that when she put his cage up to the feeding platform at the window, he would pick up a seed from the floor and hold it between the bars, and the chickadees outside would jostle one another until one had plucked the seed from his beak, and then Buddy would get another. Nellie had loved to show this off.

Eddie was glaring at me. "WHERE DID YOU THINK THEM BIRDS COME FROM?" he shouted. "We had t'have them birds ON HAND! We was feedin' a whole damn flock right through the year so Buddy could do his Christly trick two or three times a month!"

He paced back and forth by the evaporating tray grinding his teeth and glaring. "I guess I warn't upset 'nough t'suit 'er," he said. "God damn! Hasn't she got a tongue!"

One last wave of anger struck him and he howled louder than before, but there was a plaintive note in his voice and he almost addressed it to the sky.

"IT WAS NELLIE HER OWN GODDAM RATTLE BRAIN SELF OPENED THE DOOR!" he cried.

And then he calmed down. That is to say, he walked around the steaming tray panting and lurching and thumping the sides and bottom with the little stick.

He had brought some blankets in his packbasket and was planning to spend the night.

He drained off some thick syrup into a small creamery pail and set it aside to cool. He drained a little more into an old enamel frying pan and with a grunt bent down and thrust it under the evaporator tray right among the flames and coals. After it had bubbled and frothed a while, he knelt again and patted the snow, and scattered the hot syrup over it. When Shawno and I went home I had a jar of syrup for Patricia and a bag of maple taffy for the kids.

At around two o'clock the next afternoon I answered the phone and heard the voice of Nellie Dubord, whose salutation, calling or receiving, is always *Yeh-isss*, as if she were emphatically agreeing with some previous remark.

Eddie had not come home. She knew that he had taken blankets to the camp, but she was worried.

"I just don't feel right," she said. "I can't see any smoke up there. I should be able to see the chimney smoke, though maybe not. Ain't he boilin' sap? I should see that smoke too. Can you see it up there? Take a look. I guess I'm bein' foolish, but I don't know . . . I just don't feel right."

I went upstairs and looked from the west windows. There wasn't any smoke. I skied across.

There was no activity at the cabin, no smoke or shimmering waves of heat, no fire out front. Shawno sniffed at the threshold. He chuffed and snorted, sniffed again, then drew back and barked. He went forward again and lowered his head and sniffed.

The door was locked. I went around and looked in the window. Dubord lay on the floor on his back beside the little platform bed. He was dressed except for his boots. The blankets had come away from the bed, as if he had clutched them at the moment of falling. I battered the door with a piece of stovewood and went

61

to him. He was breathing faintly, but his weathered face was as bloodless as putty.

He was astonishingly heavy. I got him onto the bed, covered him with the blankets and our two coats, and skied to the road. I saw his car there and cursed myself for not having searched him for the key: the nearest house was three quarters of a mile away. I telephoned there for an ambulance, and made two other calls besides, then went back and put him on the toboggan and set out pulling him over the packed but melting trail, dreadfully slowly.

I hadn't gone twenty paces before the men I had called appeared. The two elder were carpenters, the young man was their helper. They were running towards us vigorously, and I felt a surge of hope.

But it was more than hope that I felt at that moment. Something priceless was visible in their faces, and I have been moved by the recollection of it again and again. It was the purified, electric look of wholehearted response. The men came running towards us vigorously, lifting their knees in the snow and swinging their arms, and that unforgettable look was on their faces.

Ten days later Patricia, the children, and I went with Nellie to the hospital. The children weren't allowed to go up, and Nellie sat with them in the lobby.

Dubord was propped up by pillows and was wearing a hospital smock that left his arms bare. I was used to the leathery skin of his hands and face; the skin of his upper arms, that were still brawny, was soft and white, one would say *shockingly* white.

"Sicker cats than this have got well and et another meal," he said. And then, gravely, "Nellie told me you went in for me. I'm much obliged to you."

"Did the girls like their candy?" he asked Patricia. She answered him promptly, but it took me a moment to realize that he was referring to the maple taffy, the last thing he had made before the heart attack. A few moments later he said to me, "How's my dog?" and I told him how the dog had known at once that something was wrong. A rapt, shy look came over his face.

A neighbor leaned in at the doorway, Earl Sawyer. He joined us, and after chatting briefly, said to Eddie, "Well, you won't be seein' Blackie no more."

Dubord asked him what had happened.

"I did away with him," said Sawyer. "I had to. He went after porcupines three times in the last two weeks. Three times I took him to the vet, eighteen dollars each time. I can't be doin' that. Then he went and did it again, so I took him out and shot 'im, quills and all."

Sawyer was upset.

"If he can't learn," he said. ". . . I can't be doin' that. Damn near sixty dollars in two weeks, and there's a leak in the goddam cellar. He was a nice dog, though. He was a good dog otherwise."

Sawyer was thirty-three or four, but his face was worn and tense. He worked ten hours a day as a me-

63

chanic, belonged to the fire department, and was serving his second term as road commissioner. He had built his own house and was raising two children.

"I don't blame you," said Dubord. "You'd be after 'im every day."

"He went out an' did it again," said Sawyer.

There was silence for a while.

"I can't see chainin' a dog," Sawyer said. "I'd rather not have one."

"A chained dog ain't worth much," Eddie said.

Months went by before Eddie recovered his spirits. But in truth he never did entirely recover them. I could see a sadness in him that hadn't been there before, and a tendency to sigh where once he had raged.

The change in his life was severe. He sold the new cabin he had liked so much, and spent more time in the little shed beside the house. I drove down to see him frequently, but it wasn't the same as stopping by on skis or walking though the woods. Nor was he allowed to drink whisky anymore. Nor did I always remember to bring the dog.

Most of the snow was gone by the end of that April. One night Shawno failed to appear for supper, and there was no response when I called from the porch. I called again an hour later, and this time I saw movement in the shadows just beyond the cars. Why was he not running toward me? I went out, calling to him. He crept forward a few paces on his belly, silently, and then lay still. When I stood over him, he turned his head away. His jowls and nose were packed with quills. He could not close his mouth. There were quills in his tongue and hanging down from his palate. The porcupine had been a small one, the worst kind for a dog.

He seemed to be suffering more from shame than from the pain of the quills. He would not meet my eyes; and the once or twice that he did, he lowered his head and looked up woefully, so that the whites showed beneath the irises.

I was afraid that he might run off, and so I picked him up and carried him into the house. This too was mortifying. His eyes skittered from side to side. What an abject entrance for this golden creature, who was used to bounding in proudly!

The black tips of the quills are barbed with multiple, hair-fine points. The quills are shaped like torpedoes and are hollow-shafted, so that the pressure of the flesh around them draws them deeper into the victim's body. They are capable of migrating then to heart, eyes, liver . . .

He wanted to obey me. He lay flat under the floor lamp. But every time I touched a quill with the pliers, a helpless *tic* of survival jerked away his head.

Ida was shocked. He was the very image of The Wounded, The Victimized. It was as if some malevolent tiny troll had shot him full of arrows. She knelt beside him and threw her arms around his neck, and in her high, passionate voice of child goodness re-

65

peated the words both Patricia and I had already said: "Don't worry, Shawno, we'll get them out for you!"— but with this difference: that he drew back the corners of his open mouth, panted slightly, glanced at her, and thumped his tail.

I took him to the vet the next day, and brought him back unconscious in the car.

I thought of Sawyer and his black Labrador, and saw from still another point of view the luxury of our lives. I did not go to bed exhausted every night, was not worried about a job, a mortgage, a repair bill, a doctor's bill, unpaid loans at the bank. And here was another of the homely luxuries our modest security brought us: he lay on the back seat with his eyes closed, his mouth open, his tongue out, panting unconsciously. Great quantities of saliva came from his mouth, and the seat was wet when we moved him.

•

A walk with Ida. Waldo. Persistence of the city. Kerosene light and an aphorism. The rock above the town. Wandering dogs.

Spring comes slowly and in many stages. The fields go through their piebald phase again and again, in which the browns and blacks of grass and wet earth are mingled with streaks of white—and then everything is covered again with the moist, characteristically dimpled snow of spring. But soon the sun

66

comes back, a warm wind blows, and in half a day the paths in the woods and the ruts in our long dirt road are streaming with water.

Black wasps made their appearance on a warm day in March, then vanished. This was the day that a neighbor left his shovel upright in the snow in the morning and in the evening found it on bare ground. It was the day that a man in his seventies with whom I had stopped to talk while he picked up twigs and shreds of bark from his south-facing yard, turned away abruptly and pointed with his finger, saying, "Look! Is that a bee? Yes, by gurry! It's a bee! The first one!"

But there was more rain and more snow, and then came the flooding we had hoped to be spared, as the stream jumped its banks and poured down our lower road, to a depth, this time, of two feet. For several days we came home through the woods with our groceries in packbaskets, but again the snow shrivelled and sank into the ground, and high winds dried the mud. I saw a crowd of black starlings foraging in a brown field, and heard the first *cawing* of crows. The leaves of the gray birches uncurled. There were snow flurries, sun again, and the ponies followed the sun all day, lolling on the dormant grass or in the mud. Shawno, too, basked in the sun, like a tourist on a cruise ship. He lay blinking on a snowbank with his tongue extended, baking above and cooling below. I pulled last year's leaves out of culverts, and opened channels in the dooryard mud so that the standing water could reach the ditch. Early one morning six Canada geese flew over my head, due north, silently, flying low; and then just before dusk I heard a partridge drumming in the woods.

Several days after Easter, when the garden was clear of snow and the chives were three inches high, Ida came striding into my room, striking her feet noisily on the floor and grinning.

"Wake up, dad!" she called. "It's forty-forty!"

She was seven. I had told her the night before how when she was four years old and could not count or tell time she had invented that urgent hour, *forty-forty*, and had awakened me one morning proclaiming it.

When she saw that I was awake, she said eagerly, "Look out the window, daddy! Look!"

I did, and saw a world of astonishing whiteness. Clinging, heavy snow had come down copiously in the night and had stopped before dawn. There was no wind at all. Our white garden was bounded by a white rail fence, every post of which was capped by a mound of white. The pines and firs at the wood's edge were almost entirely white, and the heavy snow had straightened their upward-sweeping branches, giving the trees a sharp triangular outline and a wonderfully festive look.

The whiteness was everywhere. Even the sky was white, and the just-risen sun was not visible as a disc at all but as a lovely haze of orange between whitenesses I knew to be hills.

An hour later Ida, Shawno, and I were walking through the silent, utterly motionless woods. We took the old county road, that for decades now had been a mere trail, rocky and overgrown. It went directly up the wooded high ridge of Folsom Hill and then emerged into broad, shaggy fields that every year became smaller as the trees moved in. We gathered blueberries there in the summer, and in the fall apples and grapes, but for almost two years now we had been going to the old farm for more sociable reasons.

After breakfast Ida had wanted to hear stories of her earlier childhood, and now as we walked through the woods she asked for them again, taking my bare hand with her small, gloved one, and saying, "Daddy, tell me about when I was a kid."

"You mean like the time you disappeared in the snow?"

This was a story I had told her before, and that she delighted in hearing.

"Yes!" she said.

"Well . . . that was it—you disappeared. You were two years old. You were sitting on my lap on the toboggan and we went down the hill beside the house. We were going really fast, and the toboggan turned over and you flew into a snowbank and disappeared."

She laughed and said, "You couldn't even see me?"

"Nope. The snow was light and fluffy and very deep."

"Not even my head?"

"Not even the tassel on your hat."

"How did you find me?"

"I just reached down and there you were, and I pulled you out."

She laughed triumphantly and said, "Tell me some more."

While we talked in this fashion the dog trotted to and fro among the snow-heavy close-set trees, knocking white cascades from bushes and small pines. Often he would range out of sight, leaping over deadfalls and crouching under gray birches that had been pressed almost flat by the snows of previous years, and then he would come back to us, sniffing at the six-inch layer of wet snow, and chuffing and snorting to clear his nose. Occasionally, snorting still more vigorously, he would thrust his snout deep into the snow, and then step back and busily pull away snow and matted leaves with his paws.

Watching all this, I understood once again that the world of his experience was unimaginably different from the world of mine. What were the actual sensations of his sense of smell? How could I possibly know them? And how were those olfactory shapes and meanings structured in his memory? Snout, eyes, tongue, ears, belly—all were close to the ground; his entire life was close to it, and mine was not. I knew that in recent weeks complex odors had sprung up in the woods, stirring him and drawing him excitedly this way and that. And I could see that last night's snowfall had suppressed the odors and was thwarting him, and that was all, really, that I could know.

After three quarters of a mile the trail grew steep. We could not walk side by side; I let Ida go in front, and our conversation now consisted of the smiles we exchanged when she looked back at me over her shoulder. I watched her graceful, well-formed little body in its blue one-piece snowsuit, and felt a wonderful happiness and peace.

Milky sky appeared between the snowy tops of the trees. A few moments later there was nothing behind the trees but the unmarked white of a broad field—at which moment there occurred one of those surprises of country life that are dazzling in much the way that works of art are dazzling, but that occur on a scale no artwork can imitate. I called to Ida, and she too cried aloud. The dog turned to us and came closer, lifting his head eagerly.

The sight that so astonished us was this: several hundred starlings, perhaps as many as five hundred, plump and black, were scattered throughout the branches of one of the maples at the wood's edge. The branches themselves were spectacular enough, amplified by snow and traced elegantly underneath by thin black lines of wet bark, but the surprising numbers of the birds and their glossy blackness against the white of the field were breathtaking.

I threw a stick at them. I couldn't resist. The entire tree seemed to shimmer and crumble, then it burst, and black sparks fluttered upward almost in the shape of a plume of smoke. The plume thinned and tilted, then massed together again with a wheeling motion, from which a fluttering ribbon emerged, and the entire flock streamed away in good order down the field to another tree.

Shawno, who had remained baffled and excluded, resumed his foraging. He stopped and raised his head alertly, then leaped forward in a bounding, enthusiastic gallop, and in a moment was out of sight. When Ida and I came to that very place, she too brightened, and with no more ceremony than had been shown me by the dog, let go of my hand and ran.

And if I had been a child, I would have followed, since it was here, at this very point, that due to the lie of the land, that is, the acoustics of the field, the playful gaiety of two voices could be heard quite clearly, a girl's voice shouting, "I *did*, Leo! I *did!*" and the voice of her brother, who was eight, replying, "Ha, ha, ha!" and then both shouting, "Shawno! Shawno!" I stood there and watched Ida's diminutive figure as she ran by herself across the snowy field toward the house that had not yet come in sight.

I looked back for a moment down the long slope of the field, towards the woods, the way we had come. I had intended to look for the birds, but our three sets of footprints caught my eye, and I couldn't help but smile at the tale they told. They were like diagrams of our three different ways of being in the world. Mine seemed logical, or responsible, or preoccupied: they kept on going straight ahead. Ida's footprints, in contrast to mine, went out to the sides here and there; they performed a few curlicues and turns, and were even supplanted at one place by a star-shaped body-print where she had thrown herself laughing onto the snow.

But the footprints of the dog! . . . this was a trail that was wonderful to see! One might take it as erratic wandering, or as continual inspiration, or as continual attraction, which may come to the same thing. It consisted of meandering huge loops, doublings, zigzags, festoons. . . . The whole was travelling as a system in the direction I had chosen, yet it remained a system and was entirely his own.

The voices of the children grew louder. I saw the dark gray flank of the made-over barn that was now their home, and then saw the children themselves, running with the dog among the whitened trees of the orchard.

These two, Gretl and Leo Carpenter, together with Ida and myself and Eddie Dubord, complete the quintet of Shawno's five great loves.

Gretl is Ida's age, Leo a year older. They are the children of Waldo and Aldona Carpenter, whom Patricia and I have known for years. But I have known Waldo since the end of World War II, when we both arrived in New York City from small towns to the west.

Aldona was evidently waiting for me. She was standing in the doorway, and when she saw me she beckoned. I hadn't planned to stop, except to leave Ida and the dog, since in all likelihood Waldo would be working, but Aldona had no sooner waved to me than the broad window right above her swung open and Waldo, too, beckoned to me, cupping his hands and shouting. Aldona stepped out and looked up at him, and they smiled at one another, though his expression wasn't happy.

Aldona was fifteen years younger than Waldo. By the time I came into the kitchen she was standing at the stove turning thick strips of bacon with a fork.

"Waldo was up all night," she said to me. "I hope you're hungry enough to eat." The large round table was set for three.

She looked rested and fresh—it was one of the days, in fact, that her entirely handsome and appealing person seemed actually to be beautiful. She wore a dark blue skirt, a light sweater-blouse of gray wool, and loose-fitting boots from L. L. Bean. Her long brown hair, that was remarkably thick and glossy, was covered with a kerchief of deep blue.

She said to me, in a lower voice, "We *are* going back."

She meant back to New York.

I had known that they wanted to. Waldo's excitement, coming here, had had nothing to do with country life. He had been fleeing New York and an art world that had become meaningless to him. His own painting, moreover, after two periods of great success, was in a crisis of spirit, and he had begun to mistrust his virtuosity. Country life had relieved him, but something was lacking, and he had said to me several times in the last two months, "We won't be staying forever . . ."

I wasn't surprised, then, by Aldona's remark. Nevertheless, it was saddening, and I knew that the loss, for Ida, would be severe.

I said as much to Aldona.

"We'll certainly miss you," she said. "All of you. All of us. But we'll be back every summer."

"When are you going?"

"Soon. I don't know."

"How do the children feel about it?"

"We haven't told them yet," she said. "They've been happy here . . . but there's so much to do in New York . . . "

I could hear Waldo walking on the floor above our heads, and moving something. I asked him, shouting, if he needed a hand. "I'll be right down," he called back.

Aldona looked into the oven. She closed it quickly, but warm air and the delicious fragrance of yeast rolls reached me.

The kitchen had been the stalls of the old barn. The ceiling was low and was heavily beamed. Narrow horizontal windows ran the length of two sides and gave fine views of our mountains, though today nothing could be seen but snowy woods and a misty white sky. Intricate leaves of plants, overlapping this way and that from suspended pots, were silhouetted against the whiteness. By the kitchen door stood a battered upright piano, on which Waldo, with his large hands, played Scott Joplin. At the far end of the room, beyond the open stairs that led to Waldo's studio, a large window was fitted with a window seat, on which were a cushion and many pillows. There were plants hanging in front of the window. A stool was drawn up to a small, neatly arranged table on which there were some books and some sheets of paper, jars of ink, tubes of paint, and an earthenware crock holding a cluster of small brushes. For two years, in this pleasant nook, Aldona, who was fluent in Lithuanian, had been translating a cycle of folk-tales for a children's book. She had done a great many *gouache* illustrations, and I knew that the project was nearly finished.

I heard Waldo on the stairs. He stopped part way down, and leaning forward called across to me, "Do you want to see something?"

After the whites and blacks and evergreen greens of the woods it was dazzling to see the colors of his work. He was noted for these colors. Color was event, meaning, and form.

Small abstract paintings on paper were pinned to the white work wall, as were clippings from magazines and some color wheels he had made recently. Larger paintings on canvas, still in progress, leaned here and there, and two were positioned on the wall for work. A stack of finished paintings, all of which I had seen, leaned against the wall in the corner.

Waldo had placed the new painting on the seat of a chair, and we stood side by side studying it. The paint was still wet and gave off a pleasant odor of oil and turpentine.

Waldo's manner was that of an engineer. Physically he was imposing. He was large but trim, with a stern, black-browed, bristly-mustached face that was actually a forbidding face, or would have been except that an underlying good humor was never entirely out of sight. When he was alight with that humor, which after all was fairly often, one saw an astonishing sweetness and charm. Aldona, at such times, would rest her hand on his shoulder, or stroke the back of his head; and the children, if they were near, would come closer, and perhaps climb into his lap.

The studio windows were sheeted with a plastic that gave the effect of frosted glass, shutting off the outside and filling the space with a shadowless white light. Beyond one of those milky oblongs we heard a sudden shouting and loud barking. Ida and Gretl were shouting together, "Help, Shawno! Help!" in tones that were almost but not quite urgent, and the dog was barking notes of indignation, disapproval, and complaint, a medley that occurred nowhere else but in this game, for I knew without seeing it that Leo was pretending to beat the girls with his fist, and was looking back at the dog, who in a moment would spring forward and carefully yet quite excitedly seize Leo's wrist with his teeth.

"It's a total dud," Waldo said dispassionately, "but

it's interesting, isn't it? Kerosene light does such weird things to the colors. It's like working under a filter. Look how sour and acidic it is. It's over-controlled, too, and at the same time there are accidents everywhere. That's what gives it that moronic look. I should have known better—I've done it before. *When you rob the eye you rob the mind."*

Abruptly he turned to me and lowered his voice.

"We're going back to the city," he said. "I'm going down in a couple of days and see what has to be done . . ."

I knew that he had not sublet his studio, which he didn't rent, but owned—a floor-through in a large loft building.

"We haven't told the kids yet," he said, "but I think they'll take it pretty well. There's so much to do there . . ."

Aldona's voice came up from below. We cut short our conversation and went down into the warm kitchen, the very air of which was delicious now with the smells of bacon, rolls, just-brewed coffee, and fried eggs.

The rosy, bright-faced children stormed in just as we sat down. Leo and Gretl clamored for juice, while Ida looked at them joyfully. Shawno came with them. He trotted to Aldona, and to Waldo, and to me, greeting us eagerly but without arresting his motion or taking his eyes from the children. "Hi. Hi," they said to me. "Hi, daddy," said Ida. All three tilted their heads, took on fuel, and with the dog bounding among them rushed out again as noisily as they had entered.

The sky was beginning to clear when I left half an hour later, and it was blue now, but a pale, wintry blue. A light, raw breeze was blowing.

I crossed the dooryard without calling to the children. They were throwing snowballs at Shawno, except for Ida, who was tagging along. Gretl hit him and shouted, "Bull's eye!" and witty Leo, throwing quickly but missing widely, shouted, "Dog's eye!" They dodged among the budded but leafless apple trees, while the dog, who did not understand that he was their target, keep leaping and twisting, biting the snowballs with swift *snaps* that reduced them to fragments.

I went alone down the snowy road to the right, toward the river. Little clumps of snow were falling wetly from the roadside trees.

I had been cheerful coming through the woods with Ida and the dog, and cheerful talking with Waldo and Aldona, though their imminent departure was troubling, but now as I walked away alone, I passed into a mood of sadness-without-a-present-cause, a twilight mood I knew to be somewhat obsessional, and that I had learned not to take so very seriously, yet often I had to pass through it to reach the solitude of my work.

My footprints were the only markings between Waldo's house and the larger road, but as soon as I made the turn I found myself walking between the muddy tracks of a car. In ten minutes I stood on the high ledge that overlooked the river.

The river was broad in this stretch, and was flowing heavily. The water was dark. Huge pieces of ice were strewn in a continuous line on the steep bank across from me. The ice had been dirty and interspersed with debris a week ago, but now the entire bank was white.

Two miles downriver lay the town, on which all such villages as ours were dependent. There were its hundreds of houses, its red roofs and black roofs, snow-covered now, its white clapboard sidings, its large, bare-limbed shade trees, all following the slopes of the hills. I could see the gleaming bell towers and white spires of the four churches, the plump wooden cupola of the town hall, also white, and several red-brick business buildings. It was a lovely sight from this height above the river, but it no longer stirred me. The town was spiritless and dull, without a public life of any kind, or much character of its own, but the usual brand names in the stores and the usual cars on the streets.

Just this side of the town, the elegant timbered latticework of a railroad trestle crossed the river high in the air, emerging from evergreens on one bank and plunging into evergreens on the other.

I had grown up in a town of hills like these. At the top of one, in the branches of a large maple, my friends and I had built a platform. I was then just twelve. I used to lie there alone at times, looking out through the leaves, dreaming of the future, except that there weren't any dreams, or rather the dreams consisted entirely of the marvelous town itself that I could see in the distance: white houses in a sea of trees, rising up in terraces on both sides of a valley. The town was larger than ours, more various, and more attractive. A white, winding highway led to it through a stunning vista of wooded hills, large pastures, and cultivated fields. To see all this was tantamount, really, to dreaming awake. If there were events in those reveries I have forgotten them, but I remember the almost painful yet joyful yearning stirred by that sight.

Halfway to the trestle before me now the hills gave way to lowland for a short distance. There must have been oxbow bends here at one time, but the river had jumped them and simplified its course, and now a sweeping arc of water bounded a large flat field. Black-and-white cows, a good sized herd, moved almost motionlessly across their white pasture toward the river.

There came a loud metallic scraping and banging from the gravel pit below me. A bucket-loader was scooping up gravel. It swivelled and showered the stones heavily into a waiting truck, that crouched and shuddered under the impact. Another truck, as I watched, drove down the long incline to the riverbank.

I went home by the same route, thinking now chiefly of the work that I had in hand.

Shawno and the children were still playing, but they were no longer running. Ida and Gretl were holding the two sides of a flattened cardboard box, quite large, and Leo, wielding a hammer, was nailing it to the rails of the broken hay wain by the house, apparently to be the roof of a hut. The dog sat near them, more or less watching. I didn't call or wave, but Shawno saw me. He responded with a start . . . and then he did something I had seen him do before and had found so touching I could not resent: he pretended that he hadn't seen me. He turned his head and yawned, stood up and stretched, dropped abruptly to the ground with his chin on his paws, and then just as abruptly stood up again and moved out of sight around the house. What a display of doggy craftiness! It makes me smile to remember it—even though I must now say that this was the last that I saw him in the fullness of his life. I did see him again, but by our bedtime that night he was dead.

I went back alone through the woods, walking on the footprints we had made that morning. In a scant three hours the snow had shrivelled and become wetter. It was no deeper than three inches now, and was falling noisily from the trees, leaving the branches wet and glistening.

At the bottom of the first hill, where I had to jump a little stream, and where that morning I had lifted Ida, I noticed a complicated track: the footprints of a deer and of two dogs. The deer had gone somewhere along the stream and then had come back, running, evidently pursued by the dogs.

Instead of going home, I turned into the little field

at the far end of which my cabin/studio was situated. Everything was quiet, the fresh snow untouched. I was halfway across the field when I caught a movement in the sky. High up, drawing a broad white line behind it, a military jet drifted soundlessly. A moment later the thunderclap of the sonic boom startled me . . . and as if it had brought them into being, two dogs stepped out of the woods behind my cabin. Or rather, one stepped out, a brown and white collie, and came toward me. The other, a solemn-looking rabbit hound, stood motionless among the trees.

I thought I recognized the collie and called to it. It came a few steps, and then a few steps more. It stood still when it heard my voice, then it turned and went back to the other dog, and both vanished into the woods.

I built a fire in the cabin, in the cast-iron stove, and spent the rest of the day at my work.

•

Before the house at night.

As was my custom, whether I had done the cooking or not, I mixed some scraps and pan rinsings with dry food and went to the door to call Shawno, who ate when we did and in the same room. Ida had come home that afternoon with Patricia, but Shawno had not.

Half an hour later, after we had finished eating, and while the water was heating for coffee, I went outside again and called him, but this time I went across the road and stood before the barn. The lie of the land was such that in this position, and with the help of that huge sounding board, my voice would carry to Waldo's fields, at least to the sharp ears of the dog. I shouted repeatedly. As I went back to the house I thought I saw movement on the woods road we had travelled that morning. I was expecting to see him come leaping toward me, but nothing happened and I went into the house.

We finished our coffee and dessert. Liza was staying overnight with the twins who had become her friends. Patricia sat on the sofa with Jacob and Ida and read first a picture book and then a story of Ernest Thompson Seton's, that enchanted Ida and put Jacob to sleep.

I telephoned Aldona. She said that the dog had left them shortly after Patricia had come in the car for Ida. He had stayed like that often with Leo and Gretl and had come home through the woods at suppertime.

I put the porch light on and went across to the barn again. I was preparing to shout when I saw him in the shadows of the road. A turbulence of alarm, a controlled panic raced through me, and I ran to him calling.

He lay on his belly. His head was erect, but just barely, and was not far above the ground. He pulled himself forward with his front paws, or tried to, but no motion resulted. His hind legs were spread limply behind him. His backbone seemed to be inert.

I knelt beside him and took his head on my knees. He was breathing so faintly that I doubted if any air was reaching his lungs. I heard my own voice saying in high-pitched, grievously astonished tones, "Oh dog, dog . . ."

I ran my hand down his body. Near his lower rib-cage, even in the shadows, I could see a dark mass that here and there glistened dully. It was smooth and soft, and there jutted out of it numerous fine points sharper than a saw. I was touching the exit wound of a large-calibre bullet.

I put my face close to his and stroked his cheek. He was looking straight ahead with a serious, soft, dim gaze. He gave a breath that sounded like a sigh because it was not followed by another breath, and in-stantaneously was heavy to the touch.

I stayed there a long while with his head on my knees, from time to time crying like a child.

I heard the front door open and heard Patricia calling me. A moment later she was kneeling in the mud beside me saying, "Oh, oh, oh . . ." in a voice of compassion and surprise.

We conferred briefly, and I went into the house.

Ida sat on the sofa, in the light of the floor lamp, looking at the pictures in the Seton book. Jacob lay asleep at the other end of the sofa.

I said to her, "Ida, something has happened . . ."

and knelt in front of her. She saw that I had been crying, and her face became grave.

I said, "Shawno has been hurt very badly . . ." I did not want to say to her that he was dead. "He's out front," I said. "Come."

She said, "Okay" quickly, never taking her eyes from mine. She gave me her hand and we went outside, into the road, where Patricia still knelt beside him just beyond the light from the porch. She was bowed above him and was stroking him. She looked up as we approached, and held out one hand for Ida, but with the other kept stroking his head, neck, and shoulders.